DARLING

DARLING

Phani Mohanty

Translated by
K.K. Mohanty

BLACK EAGLE BOOKS
2020

 BLACK EAGLE BOOKS

USA address:
7464 Wisdom Lane
Dublin, OH 43016

India address:
E/312, Trident Galaxy, Kalinga Nagar,
Bhubaneswar-751003, Odisha, India

E-mail: info@blackeaglebooks.org
Website: www.blackeaglebooks.org

First International Edition Published by
BLACK EAGLE BOOKS, 2020

Darling
by **Phani Mohanty**
Translated by **K.K. Mohanty**

Original Copyright © **Phani Mohanty**
Translation Copyright © **K.K. Mohanty**

All rights reserved. No part of this publication may be reproduced, stored in a retrieval system, or transmitted, in any form or by any means, electronic, mechanical, photocopying, recording or otherwise without the prior permission of the publisher.

Cover & Interior Design: Ezy's Publication

ISBN- 978-1-64560-078-7(Paperback)
Library of Congress Control Number: 2020939018

Printed in United States of America

To
Puspa
My Darling...
Phani Mohanty

Translator's Note

Love at the Time of Corona

While translating Priyatama I fell in love with an imaginary woman. It is a strange experience. Love has been defined by many romantic souls but the one definition I rejoice is from Shakespeare. "Love is merely a madness and…deserves as well a dark house and a whip as madmen do." I am sure the poet (Dr Phani Mohanty) has been inflicted by liberal doses of madness and his mention of dark house may suggest that he did suffer for his poetic pursuit. I did plunge in a splendid isolation even while enjoying every word he wrote about his Priyatama. Spontaneously the past invaded me and I think I have reasons to thank Smurti Patnaik (she was my classmate in my first year in college) and some other names, Sarbari, Sukanti, Sarmistha, Kanchan, Zarina, Sophia, Jyoti, Laxmi, Jina, that are perhaps fictional. However, unhesitatingly they gave their company while I was plundering the dictionary pages to spot the apt expression for what the poet has expressed so spontaneously.

T.S Eliot and some other conscientious poets have used Indian river names and some other Indian concepts in their immortal poems. I am sure the reader will enjoy some Indianness amidst the flow of love. *Bhagabatam, Sankranti, Yamuna, Atma, Parijata, Sanyasha, Sakhi,* etc. are thought-provoking concepts. Don't take *Yamuna* as a mere river and *Atma* as an imaginary Divinity. The closer you get into to these concepts the greater the warmth you get out of them and, by extension, from the flow of love.

While I was struggling to overcome the ennui of Corona confinement Lily Devi suggested that I better invest my time in translating Priyatama. I started forthwith unmindful of my resources to accomplish the task. I am happy to report that for full fifteen days Priyatama transported me to a delightful different world. Around that time I chanced upon a friend's Face Book post suggesting a collection of poems under a topical title: `Love at the Time of Corona'. The idea appealed to me because of my pleasant isolation that kept me closer to Priyatama and away from the deadly flu.

There may have been slips and shortfalls. If you find any discrepancy in the translated work you may question my ability, but, permit me to vouchsafe, you will not miss the injured masculine pride dashing against frivolous feminine caducity suffused by narcissistic lamentation. I hope fervently that you will appreciate my fanciful involvement in the subtle web of fabulous imagination. ``Aren't we such stuff as dreams are made on?'' *Kim adhikam...*

- **K.K. Mohanty**

1

Deserting me alone you left
...and you left, I am sinking and sinking
With every passing moment
In fathomless mid-ocean.

No help around...day by day
Hope shrinks,
In deep waters, alone I am
Like a man drowning to death...
I am at loggerheads with myself.

Darling, sorrow is a bluish river,
Seated on the river of sorrow
Silently I see on undulating waters
Your faded face,
In the diagram of my doom
You are a deep-dark shadow.

Plain simple attitude unattached
Lonely life,
In the sea of fog this is the day
to see a man drowning helplessly.

What all is circulating around,
With whose signal...nothing is intelligible

The parched throat is glued,
telephone dead,
the whole of sky is stuffed with intense
odour of gun powder
all news is stuffed in the
meaningless alphabet of forty-two syllables.

I am shocked...my breast swells and sinks
My Darling, every moment
in the sweetened sound
I live and die,
By the unimaginable wish of
Some sawdust un-worshipped nymph...

What? Nothing is happening in our
Material world!
Are there no overtures
In this life?
In no time some day on the river of life
There shall be tidal flow inundating
both the banks.
The contours of man's destiny shall change
like the changing hue of
the bird of all seasons;
reading on the palm some
ruthless invisible inauspicious Time
you shall flee...putting a barricade you shall...
that there will be no track to turn back...

I can't walk over the barricade
Howsoever I may try, my Darling
Can you that moment with
Cardinal passion hug my

Dust covered wrinkled pale
And elegantly emaciated body...
Wiping beads of sweat on my forehead
By your marmoreal hem...
Can you tell new tales forgetting
decade-old anguish and annoyance,
making my somber shades of sadness
freeze like unseasonal showers
and uncongealed... quietly drizzle down...

2

The four quarters and fourteen cosmoses
All feel listless, like a half-burnt wick
I lie sprawling hopelessly with my face down,

What's this life, Darling?
Every moment I beckon words and
Dismantle them
Amidst the medley of shuffled words
a sentence can't be framed in this life,

You are my only witness amidst
the Sun the Moon and countless stars,
you are my only witness - dabbling in plenty
the poet can die in hellish misery

In loneliness this life may pass
My Darling, no matter where you're
In an unreachable world, you're the
Alpha and Omega of my Alphabet,
You are my first and last syllable.

3

After the first and final felicity
You went your way, then there was no
Meeting in this life,
Like the croaking of a cracked record player
Words remained blurred and un-intelligible
At the departing moment;
Love's some forbidden tree's fruit
A full life is spent in discovering it
Amidst vilifying vitriol
Night stretches to become seven nights
In Time's blue expanses…

Will you, Darling… come
amidst this incessant pouring
Transcending skirts of long cirrus clouds,
Endless deep-blue forest
Infested with fear and fright.

Will you really come in a quiet
Afternoon with *Nupura* rhythm
Bedecked with a girdle round your waist
Jaded necklace on your neck
Adorned in gold bungles
As graceful as *Mohini*…the enchanting damsel;
After the last word I am lost

In your dream forgetting
Sin and sanity like a lovelorn
Passion-provoked *Madhaba* in lonely woods,
Bewildered I look around.
Are you really coming attired in a
Black-cloud saree, forgetting
All rasp and rancour
To the dark deep woods

On my greenish canvas-bed
The amused life-bird of my dream
Cries momentarily,
From some deep woods
Are you coming slowly-haltingly,my Darling
Your un-defiled supine frame
bent by the pressure of your bonny bazooms.

Delay no more Dear
Agile quick-silver doe-eyed,
the deep rainy regime
shall shatter my wondrous track of dreams
if God disapproves,
in your absence mind and body go dreary
and a freezing breeze blows fiercely.

4

After the last word you
Went your way, a meeting
eluded this life, after the last word
the story was never secreted,
lonely…deserted the poet perished
in helpless hell,

Gradually receding reminiscences
Get wrapped in thick mist
Suppressed smile… bated breath
And mysterious tidings…

In your leering look
Divergent scenarios
Fleet skywards
Amidst thunders of unseasonal showers

In soaked grand rainy herbal-bud
garland
Thy lithesome languid form
Resembles a lovelorn naked image
Like pellucid pearl
in snow-white apron
amorously unclad…
glamorous unparalleled like *Digambari*…

from the brush and palette
of which artist have you emerged ... you
look sparklingly blue
concealing the blue *Halahala*
in the overwhelming beverage of your beauty...

Paradise of all pilgrimage
Is your sanctified
Pious probity,

The symbol of all hope and assurance
Your sacred...
Unencumbered love.

Like an aimless navigator
Till I go round the spherical ruse of your midriff
Till I am absolutely inebriated...
And till I recompose myself

You will forgive me Dear
At the climactic moment... that is my lot.

5

How pinching it is… away from home
To float in streaks of dreams
To fly wandering in a cloud-clad sky
Quietly like a bird

How pinching it is to pine…
Lost in your repertoire,
Glued in your love…
Waiting for you
in a quiescent afternoon in sweet startle.

Stirring the memories
Moaning and groaning
Reading one's own chart of doom
To collapse like a dead stump
In unknown fear and fright.

Years have passed since you
Left with your assurance to come,
Can you count the years?
In fleeting moments I see your silhouette
Crisscrossing the *Tamala* vine,
My throat gets sticky with thirst,
There's none nearby
But anxiety caused by

By your delay has pilloried
My body and mind...

Come or not *Sakhi*
Sentimental moon-bright maiden,
Pangs of privation pester me momentarily,
Overthrowing decency...
Which woman caresses and kisses time and again,
And which woman indulges in boisterous orgy?
In your absence Dear,
The ten spheres look gloomy,
And my mind refuges to entertain
Lavishness and luxury.

Promising me to come
You have left...and just left,
Can you guess how many
Years have chugged out meanwhile?

6

Perched at a safe distance,
Do you think I'll stand with
My palms held open eternally like
a mundane mendicant
praying for your mercy?
And eternally losing my path in the maze of words
shall become uncontrollable
and despite ill-luck shall
indulge again and again in self-fight
all through my life?

I am debarred from going to war
My Dear, I am denied to take *Sanyasha*
I am restrained from falling in love
With another glamorous dame
and I am cautioned not to write poetry.

After becoming a poet has anyone
the audacity to watch him out?
Neither wife nor lover,
Nor any obsolete sacred text…
Or some outdated hoary grammar?

All theories go awry
After one becomes a poetic,

Epicenter of all exceptions is the poet...
The poet's seer
The poet's creator
The poet's *the* Almighty
Don't draw restrictive tri-lines
with your own hand,
The poet is a unique species
among all created beings.

What's this travesty, Dear?
One who you make your own at
The first sight locking him freely
In your outstretched arms suffused with
love, affection and sympathy;
can a woman strangle him
gruesomely, brutally in broad day-light
without weighing the pros and cons
just by her indiscretion...

All this is Fate, Dear
Only Fate...
To born a poet
To live and die a poet
To love an alluring ingénue
And suffer all through life...
All this is predestined, Dear
All formidable Fate.

7

Shall coiffeur your braids with flower
Shall give you floral bouquets, armlet
for your arm, tie silver anklets
to your feet,
in your *Tamal* foliage body,
my mind and body are juxtaposed,
no escape route is seen;
in the rain-laden sky
unseasonal storm flips its wings.

In this stormy night *Sakhi*
The mind moans and groans,
In giggling wintry winds
My breast's dancing
With restless breath,
Who will comfort me giving a
palliative kiss…

My whole being is offered
To thy divulging *Padmakoraka* – Lotus bud –
glamour,
Listen to the rhythms with jingle…clinking
in your warbling anklets,
Come once…merge
 in me in passionate ecstasy,

casting aside all trepidation and reticence,
in the deep bower
in stormy- wintry night,
Can body's biology care for
customs and law and restraints;

Unlinked to the body
Mind is a meaningless concept…
In the bones and joints
of your thick fleshy thigh, rings in
the scaring howl
 of the formless ghost…

How lonely I feel amidst
the bubbling crowds,
how forlorn I feel
alone… without you in the
Tamal grove…
Are you indiscrete and one with
My body made of
the five elements?
In your absence by my side there floats
In several hues
your silhouette in my mind's mirror,
In your absence truly do I feel frightened
In the unexplored soulless green thicket.

Ah, when will you come!
In anxiety I keep waiting for you
Like an adamant child in a single pursuit,
Come you may or may not…
This life is not the ultimate life…
Shall I keep waiting for you life after life.

8

Which name shall I cajole you, Dear?
Shall I call you Shyama, Sutapa, Visakha, Kanta,
Manorama
Or, Pushpa, Vithika, Bhadra
Mallika...Tilottama...

Any name I choose echoes
Your name...
In nerves and artery of my system...
In the sweet cycle after sixty-four
Summers vibrates your endearing call
Moment on moment
In the frolicking air,
Are you, Dear, the dreamy amaranthine
in some unseen, unreachable world...and
In each of my blood molecule
pulsating painful tune?

In the Konarka of thy body
I am a mute, distraught icon
That looks so bounteous but
pitiful in the mundane mutability...
in the invisible vortex our existence
seems meaningless,
pallid, mutilated...faded.

Once in a while from faraway remoteness
You appear like an
Affectionate mother,
Once in a while you appear like
a delicately touchy wife...and
when you appear
I forget plethora of Gods, Goddess
The Sun and Moon, forget I mother's
endearing soft and sweet call
Forget the predetermined Destiny...
Uncertain yet, unalterable, firm
Future...and
like a virile masculine man
All my inabilities;
Be it in love or in aversion...
my left-over remaining life
is tagged to your love alone.
.

9

Ah, it's severe suffocation
Day by day in your world
All visible vanish in a trice
In some topmost secret pinnacle,
All portraits look horrible, coal-black
Like hopeless negatives
In the luckless poet's periphery.

Leaving the poet's realm
Like congenitally dispassionate…
Life is lived here and there
Like a shadow chasing you,
Fleetingly floored face down
with limbs sprawled around

How marvelous, mysterious is thine world
Dear, stuffed with eerie silence around,
Like lines drawn on water…shafts
sharpened with envy
and jealousy dart hissing from all quarters.

How cute…profusely fascinating my sweetness
How conspicuously bewitching…delectable,
Wearing diamond anklets; sending wavy
Ripples in his ruddy childish lips

My conclusive bony baby is pestering for a
Colour television,
In flickering lamp light
In the dark dreadful chamber
My aged mum in her broken voice
Is chanting the lines of the tenth canto
(of the *Bhagabatam*) tunefully.

In village, homestead land of three generations
Land and house and mango grove
Ever neglected weed-infested fish pond
The marshy tract infested by
Strewn leaves of dense thorny bamboo,
the *Samkranti* festival , congregation of
Dola festival, all are there but to
No effect like a gentle unconcerned
polished life; all four quarters,
all ten spheres look faded and foggy
like the singed face of a just-rendered widow.

A lot of things were there to tell,
With open mind in the *Tamal* grove,
Now no zeal to say a word…
It feels like suffocation,
After passing of year after year
Indulging in your memory.

When all is lost all on a sudden
In a moving crowded train
What is there left out…
Like a skinny old man fiddling
His stick around
Shall stay put waiting hoping by chance

You will come this wrong way
Losing your path…

After everything goes topsy-turvy
In the holocaust
Only a bit of reminiscence lingers on
In some alcove, niche and receptacle
To insensate the heart,
With happy smile bid adieu, Dear
bye-goodbye for life after life.

10

No day
No night
My mind bubbles
Thinking of you

To me the fourteen worlds
Appear dark…
Because you are not with me,

Life seems oozing out
Every moment, everywhere
Your astral shadow is giggling,
It seems I am possessed…
I feel so in the high noon,

Donning a hibiscus garland on my neck
I dance and keep on dancing
Night and day doused in your remembrances

Telling me nothing
 like a homing bird
dashing to her nest
you departed…
can you recollect
how many years it has been?

Can you recollect
The day, date, star and
The Zodiac of that departure?
Can you remember
Where Saturn had rested
in my birth chart,
in which house, which radius?
Which God's command was that
That like an outdated letter
You should languish abandoned
At the corner of a web-infested
Room with your face down
in a tin casket
that had been once your very own,
very dear to you.

Who should I bare my heart out, Dear
Everyone in the mortal world
Like a damaged ship of sorrow
Is floating on the river of depression,
Disregarding time and occasion
Frozen thick darkness is speeding ahead,
earth beneath by feet is shaking;
I a clueless lover…a maverick
Though of obscure lineage am
tied to your love through eternity.

11

Bypassing time, ignoring odd-hour
Your un-bodied portrait
Glide and stand opening
my closed window,
in the soft-light wind
your sweet sonorous voice
come floating,
fragrance of body-smeared
stale turmeric fills the space,
like bubbles in water words
conspire to make tip-tip rhythm
in meaningless monologue,
my listless day and time
taper off unceremoniously.

Days pass mind pines
tales see no end,
A whole life time seems
Inadequate for one word to blend,
The mind gets restless
For you to live with you
countless ages.

Oh Dear, what's this
Irresistible wish

Whose beginning and end,
Nothing is known,
A life time is not enough
To gather all about you…
A deathly blow I survive
Only…only for you.

Time was when there was some
Relevance of my idiosyncrasies,
Tearing fetters of myriad
Illusions I rushed to you
Ignoring all etiquettes
Like one maledicted in love.

Meeting you face to face
May have a word with you,
Enquire your wellbeing,
Now a life of aloofness –
Living lonely…
what's more painful?
That you should inflict so much
Privation in this life.

Lovelorn lonesome life
Overwhelmed with grief
Is weeping with locks rumpled
a dirge…perched in
some dense twigs
In this imprecated life, is there
Anyone to give some soothing tidings?

Whatever I look for and long for
Plucking flowers,

Breaking twigs
Churning broken and benign words
All are worthless ina pathless woods,
Life is meaningless bereft of
Words in your absence.

Dear,
Wherever you may be placed
In whichever state of
penury and plenty,
words never stay hidden,
tales are like verbal arrows
they swish past miles and miles
in avuncular air.

With this mind and body
One who goes never returns…
Disquieted, the whole night is spent…
The whole night dreaming of you,
I lie afflicted
With a weary mind and body.

12

Adorned with strings of lilacs
Your glazing bun glistens,
Come, come closer and sit
Huddled with me, observe awhile…
how pale and faded looks
my face that was once
so dear and delicate to you
like the moon's dazzle.

Bedecked in magenta buds your
Your bun looks ravishing…refreshing,
Your saree is magenta-bright,
How dear to me
your entire body
Wrapped in maroon-bright saree.

In the ruined garden of
My mind you are a carefree
Forget-me-not, blooming
In the evening to wither
Next morning, come sit by me,
Speak tidbits to me with open mind;
Aren't you the only ever-burning
Lamp of love in my
Tortured existence…

13

Are you the comely cloud
Floating layer on layer,
Appearing so alluring
 in life and even in death,

Are you a pathless
Alien song bird flying alone in the
Cloud-laden turquoise sky,
Without you how deserted
Has become
The poet's paradise.

In the Memory's floral firmament
You are the rosy queen,
Tucked in your bun a
Flower of magenta hue,
And daubed in deep red lotion
With overflowing turmeric fragrance,
 like unseasonal cloud you appear
so cool and composed.

Untie your bun, Dear,
In the first flush of *Asadha*
Handy harvests of pearl
May glide on your deep black

Cascading tresses,
The dense rainy Eagle darts in the sky,
Earth's aroma issues forth
tearing the crust of land surface,
 both mind and youth are excited
Come dear, my darling,
Shall tuck a flower on your untied bun;
Unforgettable are our reminiscences…
On the river of life floats
An unhindered
rudderless ship of sorrow.

14

Your reminiscences
Come floating like solid deep dark clouds
Amidst torrential *Shravana*
From some far-off woodlands, bowers

Why this strange feeling…
When you suddenly bump
Into my mind,
Pressure shoots up in my blood,
My emaciated body looks pale…
Paler…the mind refuses to reconcile,
It pines…and pines,
The aroma of the rain-ravaged earth
Quietly eats into my longevity.

In earth's aroma
And in the sky moistened
By your fading memories
Like the lightly fleeting cloud
My life bird flies afar
Leaving my burnt out body,
Feathers fall and feathers
Sprout but the path never
Ends, scaling from sky to sky
In the timeless space
your memories overflow in air.

Chilly breeze blows in pouring *Shravana*,
Dancing its weary wings in bizarre fashion,
In the skies sparkle sober cloudy eagles
Seen bashfully with coy eyes
The tormented earth of yours and mine
Seems so disfigured like
A woman in widow's apparel.

I cannot stay under my grip
If suddenly *Shravana* sets in,
Sounding thunderous beagle…
Stimulating my blood,
impulsively I go out of my bounds,
Your reminis cences are like
The shining plumage of a
Trackless mynah;
The elemental pot is
Wallowing in earth…
In the sky there stands
The listless Lord in trance.

Your thoughts flow in myriads…
You are my dreamy *Parijata*,
On the banks of the *Yamuna*
The sandy bed withers
Waiting for the tingle of
Your anklet.

15

Look which way you may
Silver moon light's scattered
On the ground like your
Shining ivory saree
Lolling on the floor,
In the preserved bower
beyond the shrub-infested
Hill, amidst the song birds' warble
And swish and the hyena's roar,
And ear-bursting
orchestra of grotesque music ,
behind the dense, leafy banyan tree
you look so gorgeous
in moon light adorned in
Mohini's apparels.

I am weighing plethora of thoughts
From heaven to Hades
On my own am chuckling
and weeping, the very next moment
am convulsing from top to toe
overtaken by some
unknown sadness, like an
apologetic player shriveling…sinking
having made a wrong move

before hundreds of spectators,
and events occur in his mind
one after the other chronologically.

In the cycle of events,
On a pale brown candid screen
Things committed to happen or
Not to happen…
happen nevertheless,
but you are not extant
in the seven-isle global circles,
no trace of your is heard
in the deep-dark *Tamal* groves.

Howsoever I try to spot you
straining my eyes, your shade
remains elusive nevertheless
in the moon-lit deep woodlands,
I get exhausted looking around…hoping
I may unexpectedly
Stumble on a piece of your lost anklets.

16

In whose body and soul
You are concealed, Dear
 like a shadow, imprisoned in
deceitful ruse of some egotist, impotent
person...or are you locked
in Death's deep-cool cuddle?

Words given and taken
At our first meeting, you forget,
I keep on waiting...waiting
at the sorrowful
shore of *Yamuna*...

Lying on sand-bed
My pale-blue languid body,
Plentiful moon shine in the sky,
Come...come...tarry no more
In *Yamuna*'s limpid waters
Floats,prevailing over the waves,
the jasmine of your bun
and look wherever one may
snow-bright silvery
moon light is sprinkled
all around...

17

That day you had promised me
To breathe with me
 rest of your life, Dear…
promised to huddle with me like
penumbra of the shadow to go
to Heaven, Hell or nether world,
but the day of your arrival is
receding like the elusive
lotus, the bed of roses look
lifeless in shade of creepers,
the damaged Cupid's bow is
floundered on the floor,
like the fate of the
vanquished soldier
the deep dark night of
woes is quietly devouring
our world like an octopus
without our knowledge.

The house is flung open…
Wide open untidy our
Uncared-for miserable family;
For a five-feet-seven-inch
Emerald frame… how
much attachment, anxiety and
how much affection, though!

Reduced day by day
Lost in your thought
This body looks all skin and bone,
There's none to warn…or caution
when I am back home drunk
at mid-night, none to pace
in and out in anger…none to
admonish in fair and amiable slangs …
who's there except you, Dear;

Under threat of bloody repercussion
brother and kith and kin
Raise a barricade;
Intoxicated by the wine of your love
This existence is unwanted…meaningless…

18

In your abandoned world
How many non-events are not happening!
In morning newspaper
Wordy bombs keep on bursting
with boisterous fury,

The teacup is gradually
getting cold, some invisible
Soul force is playing
in the air trudging
from this room to that,
and my son who has descended
on the notorious world
carrying trace of my blood
is parroting nursery rhymes
like a domesticated pigeon.

Dear,
Like the amber image of Buddha
calm and serene
you are fast asleep
in benign posture…locked in
the arms of some imaginary
character, or
embossed in dual posture

on some dilapidated temple wall...
where are you my Dear,
you are not in my dreamy spring forest
you are not there,
neither in the colourful Paradise,
Say once Dear,
Who you are? Who am I?
We two...where are we?

19

My tiny world I have decorated
With bonny and broken toys,
Come quickly and see at least once
If the Sun rises, this cottage shall
Show up like a blighted image.

A sorrowful serenade
Will shake the whole region;
Dear,
Is love the fruit of some forbidden tree?
The moment you extend your hand to pluck
It comes as life-long torture,
And cruel desperation life after life.

This side the serene path is deserted
And dark, that side there's
Auriferous glaze and
Deep clamour of merriment,
It's exciting, edifying mode,
In Love's *Kadamba* grove
There awaits pining like a mendicant
Lovelorn deep-blue dejected *Madhav*.

Here, this side my own shadow
Seesaws me up-and-down

like a demented body-less being,
In the invisible confluence
My blood failed to congeal,
Time of your arrival lingers minute by minute
I can't stay in my volition
The conch-blow of Death
Mutilates minute by minute
my body and soul.

If you forget me Dear,
Really the tale will taper off now,
From Life's other shore
Inflows
Soft and sonorous tunes
Tearing the breast of the
River of love
Silent waves rise in
Sullen succession.

20

How close we are to Life and Death
Dear, and our love
Is serene and salubrious
Like the pellucid autumn sky.
And like twinkling jewels
In the liquor decanter,
Your memories are
Ever-elegant on my *Chiddakasha*-
Mental firmament

In Life and Death
You are my serene sanctified
Soul-sweet song
Comprehensively do you
Mingle in my being unconditionally
deathless in death…,
gleaming and glistening
the hem of your saree.

You are my succulent floral star
Mildly you sparkle
With mealy memories…
In the blue, ashore the hilly brook,
In crystal blue *Yamuna* waters,
In *Yashoda*'s empty bosom,

on *Shramana*'s broad brows,
In the region
beyond Life and Death,
in different shades of the
invisible world,
you existed, you do exist,
and shall continue to exist
like the endless blue sphere inundating
my body,
in every atom of my mind and soul
in every layer and turn of my psyche.

By barren howling of some un-genuine
Words, my dream gets fractured,
Dear
In the rain soaked foggy autumn night,
In the reddish…deep red
sweet-less fragrance of
The balsam
The lovelorn poet's heart slips into
Dream's sweat realm.

This life is not the ultimate life
Of our incarnation…
After we depart we will
Meet some day;
Our intimacy and love
never began… nor shall it end.

21

In the smoky sky
Sings the Shehnai
the torrential *raag*,
in peculiar muse and poise
tremulous
is my cagey, air-tight
and grey mundanity.

In thin dark all around looks
pale and pallid,
Alone…struck by
Shadow of aloofness
Like a half-dead snake jitters
Our lapis lazuli of love
Pines and laments
On a rosy bed.

How much attachment, affability
For the perishable body
on the fabulous earth…?
On some non-existent empire,
Like a tempting portrait
Of some profusely prosperous Duchess
Gleaming incessantly
In the mind's mirror.

Every moment the hide-and-seek
battle of life-death is fought here,
Every moment from top to the toe
Pierces the sharpened shaft
Of torture...

In the colourful psychedelic
backdrop your
face look so frightening, Dear;
The gentle sentry in the secured garden
I pass my days in separation
Like the amorous man...the flutist
playing sixteen hundred tunes ...
alone in the mortal world...
the tenure of the rain-soaked
night ends in my waiting...

22

Unless you come, Dear
Drenched in pitch dark rainy night,
your lusty-lustrous nimble limbs
clad in profusely moistened saree,
all doors and windows of this house
will be left stark open,
everything will be lying scattered,
mind and mental mirth.

In love you have maddened me!
my faculties - knees and joints-
are getting bruised; and like the thread
In the reel,my time and stamina
Are tapering off day by day.

Dear,
Your free flowing deep black
Locks are foundered in rain-washed waters,
Beneath, the heart it is shaking…
At the base of your bosoms
Temperature is slowly
Shooting up,
Breathing – inhaling and exhaling
Are swishing this and that way
Like a fast-flying horseman, and

A leafless stump biting dust
And crashing on earth
Making a tottering sound.

In such disastrous juncture
Lack of control
Will cause everything go awry,
There will be lapses in social customs
Human conduct,
sacred texts and scriptures,
there will be omissions in the
outlines of our cartography
words and alphabets and lexicography,
the hundreds of outcaste wayward
cowherds and fair folks of *Gopa*…
see, their apparels and jewelry
and sarees adorning their supple limbs
are falling off, and the nor'wester
blowing hard in quick succession.

In the rainy sky flies
The nonchalant *Chakor* flipping
Its wings…standing in melancholic trance in
Yogic despondency my nights
Roll one by one,
And with the heat of *Halahala*
my pale grey body is
Bathed in blood

23

The tale ends today…from today
You go your way
I mine…

After the episodes end
Lamenting our fate
We will go our way
You will go your way
I… mine… alone…forlorn.

On my way I am a lone soul
Day in and out
Alone I am
Like a half-doused flickering lamp
My existence or absence may
Mean the same to you,
You will walk your way
And I mine.

After end of all narration, Dear
Which other unsaid episode
Do you wish to hear,
Unknowingly seeing
your own shadow
you shivered in fear and
beckoned with your hand so
ardently that my

trance was broken mid-way...
like the image in portrait
you stayed hidden
in pale moon light
in the *Palasha* briar.

Dear,
By which Invisible cruel dictate
This luckless came to the unreal world
With maledicted Destiny...
Neither did he like a flower spent his
days scattering fragrance,
nor, did he like the stupid gardener
in this life
could grasp the meaning of the
whispers of your subconscious mind.

In the *Palash* grove
Set my bier with your own hand
Bedecking your deep black bun
with *Palash* flower,
with free hand write
the unfinished episode of our
impious misunderstanding
that had been once
more dear to us than our
love.

The tale ends...it ends
Dear, let it end now,
From here whining Fate as your
Passage you walk your way...
I my way all alone...all alone...

24

This life is like a falling leaf, Dear
Death today means second day tomorrow
For this two-day life, how much greed
How much attachment…it's all
Blood and tears in the festivity of love.

The sick hand of moth-eaten relation
Like cobweb we were entangled
for some days,
From beginning to end there have been
many colourful festoons…
In our tiny world how much conflicts,
How many more anger-exasperation,
Calumnies…
And cruel doses of inflictions!

Every moment
the excruciating balls of fire, my bonny blonde,
is smouldering my body
that was once very enchanting to you,
every moment I am being suffocated…
wherever I look there's
thick darkness…over-stretched pitch black.

Memories thrive in the material world,
tales never die eternally

The body dies mind dries away
Hope and expectations too perish,
Love dies not...

Every moment from the
Day of your departure
This grey body feels burdensome,
How many times did I not contemplate
To end my life...
But didn't meet death only for you,
Lest you should be left alone
And break down in sorrowful load,
Accusing me smilingly you may
Tell others, "Look...look, this tribe of men,
How conceited, selfish
False, lecherous, womanizer."

I am tied to your love eternally
Dear, in life...in death
In life after death and thereafter...
if there's any certitude
To live
At any point
In every conscience
I'll live on in throes of death
Cuddling your remembrances
In the terrifying all-pervading
In eternal expectation...
In the green oasis in the slice of Time.

25

For which crime of mine
Do you prepare my funeral pyre,
While I am alive in the veritable world?

Placing on sandal-wood-bed
my five-feet-seven-inch frame, and
Offering flower and *Nirmalya*
By your both raised palms,
May you captivate the manly ghost
By chanting charmed incantations;
Concealing all sobs in your breast
Pour ghee with your own hand
Light the fiery fire to burn in rage
chained in worldly fetters
with husband and son…
Like a newly-rendered widow.
Hide your face in shame.

Everyone is curious…asking,
Tell us, oh Poet, who is
Your Priyatama,
For whom you are penning
Volumes of love poems,
Is your Priyatama, oh poet, a Deity
Made of blood and tear, or
Devil, tell once with open mind…
Better the song of life left unsung.

26

Like chicken's severed head,
this body shakes
And shivers momentarily,
Once and again I am popping up
And drowning
In the coral isle of your love.

Every moment
The sharpened arrows of jealousy
Hatred and suspicion shot
From your world of deceit, falsehood
Pierce me blood-bathing my
Sinless soul.

Burnt and ragged my abandoned
carefree mind and soul
is petrified every moment
by the curse of some
devilish deity.
Seems a bomber aircraft is
Crashing on me all in one piece…

Like a blind self devoid of
Vision undeniably do I see your
Frightening terrifying form,

in my nerves and
arteries deleterious poison is
Spreading like smouldering fire…
Your lips are unable to utter
A word, like an accused sentenced
To death without trial,
I am seeing your
All-consuming cosmic form.

27

Darling,
Our acquiescence and dissent
are they confined to a day? Is our
Sweetness a house made of
Crystal
That may crash by a little jolt?

Knowing all this
How daringly I am spending
My days stealthily here and there
Splurging your
Ever-alive reminiscences...
And my pain is surging
moment by moment
in my degenerating
invisible limbs.

If in this life
You love me, do not
Mistrust me, do not
Misread me,
Do not, by creating canards
Vilify yours and mine
Sanctified love, if in this life
You love me... envy me not

In this life or life after life,
Don't denounce my hand.

In love the poet conquers
the world, the poet
Is the lover…
Deep down in grave blue
Melancholic sky of your mind
I would be flying a lonely bird
With no fear … no anxiety…
No apprehension in mind.

28

Ah, what's this inexplicable pain
My whole body is getting fatigued
My heart is shivering as if I
Have been thrown off the space.

Am I the same destitute son
of the sentry man in the
widely known childhood fairytale
repeating the '*Sasemera*' '*Sasemera*'
mantra , I am transformed into a
cadaver beneath a tree
and am waiting unperturbed
without any complaint for
my final verdict.

Before the dawn opens up,
If in real measure
air carries news of my
Demise to you,
What plea will you take?
Will you boarding the *Puspak*,
Fly stealthily hiding yourself
to see my corpse
with the eye of a beloved?

In hate, and deep aversion
may you shed two drops
Of gleaming ruby tears
From your eyes,
Tears of your eyes are the
Only props of my remembrance
in my maledicted life.

Darling,
Emotion once ruptured
Can't be reunited again,
Once the path is lost
No support comes by
In endless eternity.

In the canorous world
Murmurs mellifluously
the *Yamuna* of love…
Nothing to lament even when
Bodily attachment
Corrodes,
I am eternally tied to your love…
Don't resort, Dear, to
Pretension in love.

29

In which unattainable
Metaphysical realm
You may relax, Dear
Be a star, dazzle in twinkle
In the blue sky,
Chuckle like a flower in
The gratifying garden.

With love preserve the
Decadent devastated world
May our love flourish to finish
In the *Palasha* paradise,
May the episode linger
Transcending time till
Eternity.

You may stay put in some
unapproachable world,
we will meet some day in
this life in some non-existent
planet, sub-planet
or some unknown continent…

Love's lore lingers millions
Of ages, tales are never
Exhausted, tales of the
passionate poet live on by
Words of mouth
Age after age.

30

Wherever you may be
In whatever milieu, call me
To your mind once
In the triadic eventide and
Plant a kiss with your pallid lips.

Forget like a nightmare
Our sightless past,
Pre-determined Fate,
All failures, and the life of
Sin and sanctity,

With Love's greenish fetters
Embrace...
The perennial soul;
Let not illusion delude
The dale of deep blue eyes, and
the disobedient... defiant poet.

Better in a ray of dazzling light
rest of life be washed away...
curse not taking pity
on our pious souls.

Wherever in whatever
state you may be
at the final hour smilingly,
like a compulsive lover,
plant a kiss on me;
Invoke the five elements,
the in-coming, out-going breaths,
smell them, touch them,
poise them, Dear overwhelmingly
in intimate embrace.

31

Don't I remember *tithi*,
date, *rashi*, *nakshatra* of that day.
Perhaps, it struck 10.30 in the
clock of the church beside our temple,
Your naked body, like a stale copse
Lay on a new model
Ultramodern teak bedstead

In the sky disorderly
Unmindful squads of floating
Black clouds were loitering
Incessantly,
The constellation of stars was fast asleep.

My slumber was fractured
In a start by a bad dream,
Sleep was broken…so
broken that howsoever I flipped
and kept on altering my side
sleep eluded me, as if a
colossal fear spiraling like a snake
on the elegant leg of our
bedstead secreted sidelong
there and was biting me

with its dangling
pitch black tongue hissing furiously.

I shuddered gripped with fear and
Anxiety seeing the fearsome snake
And the cosmic form of
the metaphysical universe
in the snake's palate.

So many awful-wonderful planets,
Unknown unheard stars, undiscovered
Rudra and ferocious streams and rivers,
Tough terrains, spiritual world,
Material world metaphysical world…
Saw numerous sights one by one
No reliable sacred text has
language to narrate them…

What's that strange cacodemon, Dear
In that frightening night stuffed with darkness,
Flowing with night's dark wave
Has a fake *Kapalika* ventured to
Enjoy your entire copse-like body.

In the pungent odour of your breath my paternal
propensity
Gets exhausted, emaciated;
Like the stony image of *Rudra*
Your blood-and-bone body
Is overwhelmed in dreams,
Like the shivering envelope sealed
With saliva of your milk-pinkish
Lips static and stationary;

But that swarthy savage
Is engrossed in ceaseless amorality,
But like disinterested
Image of divinity you
Deigned unconcerned...
Unmindful...

32

Didn't you protest
didn't you wake from sleep
Didn't blurt out aloud to
Wake up others,

Were you really past your prime carnality,
Like a hypnotized woman
Lost in pleasure did you
Lie in that sweet yet tiresome
Terrible portrait?

Burning in high rage
I roared, bit my lips,
Clenching my locks furiously
In deep anguish
I cursed your father and
Ancestors, I was trying like a
Butcher to mince the
silk thread tied with you…
to live a different life.

But, I couldn't stir
Couldn't call the neighbours
Nearby, nor could tap all the switches
In the house to see your face
Straightaway in glowing light.

My dream crashed all on a sudden
Dear, by the strange roar of your
Pet black cat, I rubbed my eyes to see
You flung like a burnt out log
on your elegant couch.

Dared I not to call you
By your name, with drowsy eyes you
Stretched your limbs to
Break the inertia, cracked your
gracile finger spopping,
Slowly then in ease and unhurriedly
Twitched and adjusted your unclothed
Prostrated frame, and asked nonchalantly
And graciously
And putting a poser:
Tell Poet, for my sake say once,
Has something untoward happened?
Did you see a useless frightening dream?

All dreams don't come true
Don't sadden your mind,
I shall be always by your side,
Like a shadow
For ages and eons after eons.

How simple and straight was your query,
And its answer,
Like a clueless statue I am
Seeing again and again
Your cool, peaceful, candid, graceful
Languid disposition.

Dear,
a grave apprehension
grips these days in my middling years,
all additions/ deductions are
going awry in the quixotic-dream
poet's spatial planet.

33

You had given your word of honour to
Come... certainly
Some day in thunder, storm...
Lightning and in dense darkness
Despite shrieks of our
Our expectant hoary world.

You will come, Dear
Inundating my nerve and nerve with
excitements of the
Material word,
Like an ordinary woman
Amidst jingling ringing resonance
In an eerie...barren moment of a
Frightful night.

You will come...jauntily attired I have been
Waiting from behind years...years
Twizzling my wrist with
A jasmine wreath, smearing my brows
With sandal paste, cleansing by body with
Haridra water, sprucing my mundane periphery
With scents of incense camphor,
Have hijacked a few moments from
My finer half for you to come;
Shivering in the scintillating zephyr

Pained in hands, bones and joints;
For one nocturnal prowl
I have arranged for you royal reception
With great grandeur ...pageantry and pomposity.

Sure, you will come in gleaming lunar luster,
There will be no storm in the sky
No rain and thunder; there will be dazzling
Festoons of light, the gorgeous visible world
Would have surged transcending horizons;
Jostling the crowded traffic you will run,
No matter how untoward things might happen.

Cheap hoardings of
Death and premature departure,
principles and ideals, probing eyes...
alert vigilance and Draconian dictates
Of social supervisors, hollow
Resonance of blemished character,
calumny, canard et al;
Sidetracking all these
You will come...
You will come someday
Negotiating
Your way through the consanguine stream,
May be even at the jiff of my
Final departure.

Like a blameless bud you will come
That's why I have kept my door open,
Tied as I am to the love of
Mother, wife and son...
I am a forlorn captive of love.

34

Profuse fragrance of daisy attar
In my embroidered blue attire,
The main gate was open whole night
Like a prisoner in watchful detention
my days pass... my nights pass
But no trace of yours I see
In the neighbourhood of
This phenomenal world.

In the far-off firmament like a blinking
Eye burns one lonely blue star,
My main gate is flung open the
Whole – the whole night.

For me writing poetry is forbidden, and
For you going around the market
Is screeched... to become worldly
Is prohibited and for you also
Prohibited to become a mystic.

Time trickles to midnight
But, there is no inkling of your coming,
The assortment of flowers has faded
And your pretence and alibi is discerned,
I don't stay under my grip, better

Time glide, better the rose bed
Get stale, better our tale and lyrics
screech to a halt here and now.

In Bramha's malediction
Inauspicious sigh,
Better this tiny nest
Be destroyed,
Better there be none by way of
Posterity to claim that his Dad
Was a powerful
Uncompromising fearsome
Hero… for just a woman
He frittered his ancestral gift…
His invaluable life.

Dear,
It's my final appeal to you
At my time of farewell for this life:
Whether you come or not I am
Not pained, may this libertine *Kanhayee*
stay on earth
inebriated in pristine love.

35

I am your dear poet,
You are poetry of my life,
Stay at any unreachable
Realm you may
I don't feel dismayed;
You are the soul of my soul,
My reflection... you are the ever-burning
Lamp in my mortal and post-death existence
Whether you grasp or not the
Play of words... our love nest is stainless,
We both are symbolic of each other.

For your cloistered comfortable life
The poet has no envy, no attraction;
The poet has no greed no animosity for
Your arrogance...egotism,
For your eternal emotive life
My tongue sings in hundred tunes,
The uncertain cycle of our
Desires-dislikes, my amplified
Manliness boasts in the
material and metaphysical worlds...
may they melt like wax, may
our emotive world-nest
get destroyed but, may there not exist

a single word to narrate
the miffed manifesto of our
secluded love.

Dear,
Instead of smouldering inside
And turning into cinders, what's
that pain that is so torturous
and excruciating in this world
of possibilities that referring to sacred
texts, altering the path of planets and
stars, in aversion, disgust, envy and infamy
you will adore your dear poet
with a torn-tattered crown.

36

In intimate caress
Gracious affection
Close tight embrace,
In warm fetters of kinship
Won't you kiss me once…
Once last time?

At departing moment
At the solemn juncture, Dear??

May none be inflicted by this pain
Even one's own enemy,
To be carried in a palanquin
Like a cadaver while full of life,
To lie spreading tired limbs
Like a half-dead fish in full view of
Onlookers,
To be bruised by the invisible
Harpoon all the while without respite,
Or entangled by web of immoderate
words of
an intentional arrogant critic,
or the unreasonable flattery
of a sycophant…
what's more shocking than to come

to public notice by being branded that
I am writing poetry being quietly
Influenced by some this or that poet…

This shock is more
terrible than death, Dear,
but how easily a poet or two of our generation
are condemned to singe in
self-condemnation
till they just disappear.

Oh, what misfortune! what
Misfortune, Dear!!
In the material world.

37

Did I ever imagine
Such a catastrophe
could happen while
I was on way back home
Lost in your thought?

That I would overturn
Like a tree laden with fruits
And flowers, that
In a trice there would be
Din and bustle in your whole
Residential unit, that
There would be a melee
At accident site with unknown people
Rushing in… that some
neighbourly woman would
pour a sip of water in my mouth
and wipe sweat and saliva on
my face and brows with her hem,
like a veteran doctor someone
would feel my pulse and shout;
"Get a taxi, call the ambulance",
Or someone else sobbing would lament
That this man walked everyday this way
By my house, never utters a curse

Even to a fly; look what's his ill luck...
He had to suffer so grievously
For no fault of his, his wife would be
Waiting for his return... once outruns his time to
Get back she would pace in and out
In her house, and would be trembling
With unanticipated anxiety.

Oh, who's where, come running
Come, pour a drop of water in
His mouth, his throat has dried up
Like glue, his diary and pen are
Dashed off there... oh, see if his
Home address is written
On his diary page... ring his home,
Call the doctor, note down...
the trekker number it might be of use
when occasion demands.

How blatantly so many meaningless
Words were misused, Dear, right
In my presence, the onlookers
next moment bid their time
and finding their direction
went crisscrossing their own way.

Amidst so much noise and cacophony
How was I gasping to hear for once
That forgotten moistened symphonic voice;
How desperate was I to hear that ten years ago
While roaming with you
Stealthily in your unit
In a rickshaw.

38

Had I anticipated the impending
huge disaster on way back home
I would have, half way, taken a detour...
Would have stopped my scooter
Abiding by traffic rules, the inauspicious
Accident hour would have passed
During my wait, there would have been
no traffic snarls on streets.

Like days in past I would have returned
exactly at 2.30 p.m.,
my cute-comely sweet heart would have waited
at the front corridor of my house
eagerly expecting my return.

Never, even by mistake,
in newspapers, it would have
been printed in bold prints
That the poet of 'Priyatama'
Is no more in the mundane world... he fell
To premature death in collision
With a trekker owned by a private company.

Wherever you may be Dear,
in whatever state... this sad news

would have reached you some day...
like the odour of a burnt out cadaver
playfully transiting in the air.
Though not in love...in disgust, outrage
In compassion... a drop of tear
would have oozed out of your
deep azure eyes much
against your will.

Deep down... in the inner self meteors
Would have bombarded the
Innermost corner of your heart
Like bolt from blue,
Dirges would have filled all
Air and ether, all ten quarters
would have worn a
Deserted look in the sequence
Of events, the poor mindless
adamant poet would have lain
as an unidentified copse
at the turn of the road running
in front of your house.

39

After the accident I was hurled out
In a blink of the eye at such a spot…
It seemed as if a star was dislodged
From cosmic firmament,

Hundred scorpions' sting
In my body, around me are
smoky dense
Mountains replete with layers of
Clouds, mid-sea the rudderless
Dented-damaged canoe of life,
No shore to be seen no anchor…
No one by my side to tell about
You; are you gone or alive?
Or clad in a blue saree of some
Unseen autumn…sporting around your
Neck a string of sapphire
enjoying reckless
Sex with some swarthy bod at this
Time of grave crisis.

If news of my departure reaches you
Floating in windy chariot while
You are in full flurry of coition,
what will you do,

Dear? Will you end your life
Sucking the diamond nugget?
Tearing off cloths, ornaments from your
Gold-gleaming body, will you
Like a mental case sob and weep on road side?
Or pouring out your mind
To your timid man shall rush
To see my lifeless copse once for the last time;
Placing a gardenia wreath you will mutter to
Yourself: Oh, Poet, how naughty deceitful
Adamant lecher debonair you had been!
A bit of tiff and taking umbrage you left
In a huff…you left and didn't
Look back even once at me.

Who will fathom your heart, Dear
The psyche is like the onrushing current of a
Swelling river… breaching dam and defense
It intrudes far and farther.

The body may perish any
odd moment in this terrestrial world…
The Soul-bird is ever blithe and
buoyant for eons, and
more delectable than death is our
love and our Elysium of love.
.

40

Forget not a small supplication
At the exit hour, no matter what's
The infliction have no ill-will for the
Departing soul, withering in silence
Don't indulge in self-mutilation,

In *Swargadwar*
On sea shore
In the medley of people
Prepare my funerary
With scented sandal wood,
I would be lying in deep slumber
facing the South, cerulean waves of the blue sea
would glide up undulating crashing their head
on sand dunes… sweet lute tunes
would be audible from nearby
hundred, hundred miles.

Sleep, no matter in which
Direction 'Darling' the music 'Darling'
Would float from air… water… ether
Earth's aroma,
No regret… if not in this life,
In some invisible birth
We will meet in seclusion…

on moon-lit *Yamuna* waters
at a time when two un-embodied *Atma*
are lost secretively in furtive boating
at jetties and river edges
in gleaming full-moon night...

41

After cremation
Generously from your self-earned
Fund, treat to best of
Your ability the destitute
Poor and beggar
And Brahmins
with a sumptuous feast,

Announcing I was a fatherless son
Don't pray for help from
friends relations
Kith and kin,
Observe solemnly
Obsequies, feed the poor
Give alms and perform other tidbits
Ceremoniously according to custom;

Very affectionately
Scatter my ashes at every square,
Lane by lane in every unit
Of our dear city;
No matter from which side you come
Jingles of anklets worn on
Your feet would ring in my ears.

42

Forget not my last supplication
At my departure:
Never entertain sinful thoughts
Never tell anyone…
Even yourself
that once you had betrayed me.

Rest of your days
Cheerfully run your show
Hold all together cordially
With care and affection.

Rare is human birth, Dear
From previous births' good deeds
It comes by once a while as a result
Of boundless virtues,
Once the palm gets exposed to Eternity
It flies like a cage bird
into azure heavens,
Howsoever wailing… lamenting
It is never seen again in the
World's seven-territorial isles.

May be there's previous life,
May not be; this is the last
life of Love-lust envy-hate

Attachment-affection;
In this life we have to endure the current time,
the future heaven-hell
sin-virtue discord-differences
freedom and fetters,
.
This life's
everlasting-pure-enlightened-unfettered-eternal
and truth-endless.

Even in dream never forget
My last supplication at
My departure,
In deluge even if our love-laden
Canoe is devastated to extinction
I shall do *japa* of your name, Dear
For millions of ages and eons…

Glossary

Atma-	The subtle divine life force in all living beings, roughly equivalent to what is called Soul.
Asadha & Shravana-	the rainy season
Bhagabatm-	One of the most sacred religious of texts read routinely in devout Hindu households
Brahma-	The Creator. Both his benediction and malediction are potential
Chakor-	The singularly unfortunate bird. Howsoever they are in love the male and female are debarred from spending the night together
Digambari-	Goddess Durga who appears most amazing both for her grace and fury
Dola-	The festival of colour involving Lord Krishna who plays with His friends and devotees syringing coloured water on each other
Gopa	the mythical village on Yamuna sacred for being witness to Lord Krishna childhood lila
Halahala-	The deadly poison that Basuki, the cosmic serpent ejected while serving as the churning rope at the time of churning of the Ocean. Hemlock of Socrates' reference could be its near equivalent.
Haridra-	a hard-crust brown-colour solid fruit that has curative qualities.
Ishwar-	The Lord Almighty.
Kadamba-	A bulky flowering tree with ball-shaped enticing

	flowers that are dear to people in love. There are several mention of Kadamba on Yamuna shore where Sri Krishna roamed and played with his friends
Kanhaye-	One of Sri Krishna's most affectionate names
Kapalika-	A practitioner of violent weird rites with human corpses and skulls to assume supernatural power
Madhava-	One of the oft-remembered numerous names of Sri Krishna. For a lovelorn poet Madhava is a symbol of hope.
Mohini-	Vishnu's female incarnation at the time Ocean churning. She appeared as a most captivating woman and the demon participants in the churning were so enamoured by her beauty that they just fell for what She suggested. In the current context Mohini is singularly beautiful.
Nirmalya –	The dried grain that devotees of Lord Jagannath partake as a purifier of sin.
Narka-	The hell as described in Hindu philosophy. The region where the departed soul is tortured for its misdeeds.
Nupura-	Dancers' anklet fixed with tinkling nuggets to rhyme with background music.
Padmakoraka-	The unfolding lotus bud that gradually divulges the full glory of the flower
Parijata –	The divine flower of Amarabati, the Gods' abode. It may be imagined as a flower that holds magical hope for a lovelorn.
Patali –	A flower of maroon hue that is lovers' choice. Lilac comes closer to its description.
Palasha –	A typical flower symbolic of pain.
Puspaka-	The mythical aircraft of the demon king Ravana as referred to in the Ramayana.
Rudra-	An oft referred name of Lord Shiva who is worshipped with *Brahma* and Vishnu as the Supreme Trinity in Hindu tradition
Sakhi-	Perhaps the most sanctified endearing name a lover gives his lady love

Sankranti-	The first day of a Hindu month considered auspicious
Sanyas-	Renunciation – Seeking peace in mental seclusion by withdrawing from worldly activities.
Sasemera-	An episode involving the great poet Kalidasa; it tells of man's ingratitude to a wild animal that sheltered him from sure death.
Shramana-	A devout Buddhist monk who practice the Fourfold path in search of Nirvana
Swargadwar-	The Gateway-to-Heaven crematorium in Puri, the earthly abode of Sri Jagannath. Here scores of corpses are consumed by fire twentyfour hours a day to get a sure passport to heaven..
Tamala-	An enticing flower.
Yamuna-	The polluted river seen today was the mythical limpid stream that is witness to Lord Krishna's childhood pastimes (lila).
Yashoda-	Sri Krishna's doting mother in Gokul
Yogini-	The female semi-Goddess having supernatural power. A Yogini can take her devotee to a great height in the material world.

■

www.ingramcontent.com/pod-product-compliance
Lightning Source LLC
Chambersburg PA
CBHW021128080526
44587CB00012B/1180